MW00779994

Effective communication skills:

Table of Contents

How to Persuade

It takes great skill to convince others to see things the way that you want them too. This technique is commonly referred to as the art of persuasion. You're not forcing them to go along with and accept the new ideas that you're presenting, you're simply honing in on your communication skills to persuade and convince them to come around. Marketers and advertisers use this all the time, even salespeople do sway customers into making a purchase from their business. Certainly, the art of persuasion is a valuable skill set to possess, but how do we learn to harness those powers of persuasion?

Persuasive communication is about shaping someone else's belief, to convince them that your idea is the one to go along. Persuasion, however, is going to need more than just your ability to be able to mold someone else's thoughts and opinions. To convince them enough to take action based on the ideas you have inspired them to do, that's going to require you to create a sense of certainty, conviction, and belief. You're going to have to make them feel confident enough that your approach is even better than the ideas that they might have.

Is It Possible to Change Someone's Mind?

It is if you know the right approach and the techniques that you need to use. We have all experienced those moments of frustration when you were in a heated argument or debate with someone and they simply refused to see things from your point of view. You thought you were doing everything you could to get them to see you were right, yet they obstinately refused to budge, and it seemed the more you tried to "convince" them, the more obstinate they became.

Trying to convince, persuade or change someone's mind is challenging. Perhaps the problem lies with the approach that we use. Most people tend to lead with their own point of view and their own perspectives and then proceed to point out what the other party needs to do to change. This approach hardly ever works the way we intend it to because it makes the other party defensive, even personally attacked when they're being told all the ways that they're "wrong" and why they need to "change" according to you. Effective persuasion requires an entirely different approach. You need to take a step back and rely on empathy to understand where the other person might be coming from. Nobody likes being told they're wrong, and they especially don't like to feel as though they're being forced to change. That is why a subtler approach to persuasion is going to be far more effective. Arguing and debating the pros and cons with them is only going to get you so far, but offer very little chance of successfully convincing them to change or go along with your point of view. Empathy and the ability to understand the other person's concerns, validate their emotions and then working together with them to arrive at an outcome both of you would be happy and comfortable with is the very best way to change someone's mind.

The art of persuasion is not just about telling the other party what they should or shouldn't do. If you want to truly persuade them, and convince them to believe in what you're telling them so much they're willing to take action, you're going to have to:

- Earn Their Trust - No one is going to be convinced by anything you say if they, first of all, don't trust you. The more familiar you are with the person you're trying to persuade, the easier they will be to convince. Trust breeds the willingness to perhaps consider changing their point of view, and if you're in a situation where you're pressed for time to build trust, try building your case instead based on credible or reputable sources that are known to be trustworthy.
- Learn What Matters to Them - If you want your message to truly resonate with someone, you need to speak to them where it touches them the most. By talking about the issues that matter and what's important to them.
- Offer a Guarantee - If you're absolutely sure of what you're saying, go out on a limb and reassure the person by offering some kind of guarantee that would make them feel better about changing their mind. An example of this would be if you were trying to convince the team at work to go along with your suggestion and you were 100% confident it was going to work out, a "guarantee" to convince the others might look something

like this: "Trust me, if my idea doesn't work, I'll bring donuts in for the entire team for a month!".

- Make Them Believe the Idea Was Theirs - People are easier to convince when they believe that they arrived at the solution on their own. Even if it was through your gentle guidance that steered them in the right direction, let the final decision rest with them, allowing them to believe that it was their idea all along. One effective approach would be to get them to list the pros and cons, and then asking them which they believe would be the best approach to take from there.
- Agree with Their Opinions - Since nobody likes to feel pressured into doing anything, you'll have an easier time convincing them if you agree with their perspective every now and then. During the conversation, whenever they raise their concerns, agree with them by saying "I can see your point, and I agree that this is a cause for concern. However, I do believe…". Validating their feelings lets them know that how they feel matters to you, and that you're not simply

trying to cram an idea down their throat for your own benefit.

The Art of Persuasion

If you want to convince others, you need to first have that same belief and confidence in the ideas that you're trying to transmit. The art of persuasion relies not just on what you say verbally, but it is a combination of both your dialogue and body language abilities. Almost every interaction these days requires some form of influence to take place. Direct sales, marketing, advertising, job interviews, client meetings, business dealings, the need to influence is all around us. It is how we work with others to achieve the goals we have in mind. To achieve success, this is one skill that you're going to need in your arsenal.

Persuasion is situational. The techniques that work well in one context might not be as effective in another. To pull it off, you're going to have to rely on a multitude of communication skills. Standing up tall, speaking with confidence, charm and pose alone is good, but if you want to take things up a notch, your body language needs to be as strong as your verbal language, and they need to work well together. You're trying to convince your audience, and your body language has to resonate that just as strongly as your words do. Imagine if you were trying to convince a client why your service package is going to be the best value for their money, but your body language conveyed nervousness all throughout the discussion. You were nervous, jittery, sweating slightly and had a hard time maintaining eye contact. Even though you were saying all the right words the client needed to hear, your body language would be throwing them off and they would still walk away from the meeting with uncertainty.

The art of persuasion needs confidence, surety, and the following techniques to be considered effective:

- Stand Up Tall - The most basic rule to looking confident (even if you may not be feeling like it) is to stand up tall, with your shoulders back and maintain good posture. Slouching, unfortunately, has become a habit that most of us a guilty of and one that is hard to break, but in the art of persuasion, a confident posture is an absolute necessity. No one is going to be convinced in your idea if your shoulders are hunched and you're slouched the entire time since it makes you look less than confident when you do. Straighten up and stand up tall. Not only will you look and feel a lot more confident when you do, but the correct posture also helps to align your airway, which then enables you to speak louder and clearer. A sure-fire way to appear even more confident.
- Don't Be Too Stiff - Standing up tall and maintaining good posture doesn't mean you should be rigid when you do. If you're up on a stage, make full use of the space available to you and move about freely, but naturally. Even if you happen to be giving your address behind the podium, move about freely and use the available space

around you. Many speakers often make the mistake of just standing behind the podium the entire time, but the speakers who are the most successful at leaving an impact on their audience are the ones who move about freely and with ease. They are the ones who appear more confident and at ease with their surroundings, and this allows the audience members to be more receptive to them. Think of the last time you were in a speech where one speaker just stood stiffly in one spot while the other moved about. Which speaker stuck out more in your mind?

- Open Up - Keeping your posture open is important in the art of persuasion. Not only does this make you look confident, but an open posture signals to the person you're speaking to that you're trustworthy, even if this is only happening on a subconscious level. People who seem "open" are often associated with having nothing to hide, and when you're trying to persuade another to go along with you, you need to make it clear that they can trust you. No one is going to be convinced by someone they have a hard time trusting. Avoid folding or crossing your arms in front of your chest, or putting your hands in your pockets when you speak. Convey openness by keeping your palms exposed and facing up, and keep your limbs relaxed and as open wide as possible to demonstrate that you're someone who has nothing to hide.

- Look Them in the Eye - Eye contact has been mentioned several times already, and it makes another appearance here in the art of persuasion because maintaining good eye contact is so crucial in any form of communication. Eye contact is as much a key part of the communication process and body language as interviews are when you're trying to get a job. Good communication cannot exist without good eye contact, it is simply not possible. You're going to have a hard time trying to persuade anybody if you can't even look them in the eye. They're going to think something is up or there's something fishy going on. Looking at your audience in the eye is easier when it's a small group of people, or if you're having a face-to-face conversation. If you're in a much larger crowd, however, since looking at every single audience member in the eye is going to be impossible, focus instead on the key members sitting in the audience and focus instead on maintaining good eye contact with them. They'll be easier to convince when you do.

- Relaxing Your Facial Expressions - When it comes to assessing trustworthiness, the area that we often focus on the most is the face. This is where most of our attention is focused on, and even when you're standing up on stage in front of a large crowd, that doesn't change. Your audience is still going to be searching your face for signs to clue them in about your intentions and how honest you seem. To be thoroughly convincing and persuasive, your facial expressions must match what you say, and your expressions must look relaxed and natural when you do. Trying too hard is going to make you look like you're faking your expressions, and audiences will be on the lookout for any kind of indicator that might give them a reason to doubt your credibility. The art of persuasion can only be effective when you appear to be someone that others can trust.

Now, the techniques above are good for when you're speaking to an audience whilst your standing, but what if you were sitting down during the conversation? How would you apply the art of persuasion to appear just as convincing when you're seated in one position? Not all speeches are going to require you to be in the standing position. In business meetings, you might be sitting down. When you're negotiating with a client, you might be sitting down. Even when you're among family and friends, a lot of conversations are likely to take place when you're sitting down. Pulling off persuasion from the seated position is still possible, and you'll need to keep the following techniques in mind when you do:

- Don't Get Too Comfortable - When you're trying to convince the person you're speaking too, allow them to get comfortable in the chair. You, on the other hand, need to refrain from getting too comfortable, since you're going to have to demonstrate passion and enthusiasm, and you need to look engaged when you're speaking. Sit slightly more upright to appear more confident, and lean forward in your seat when you're speaking.

- Still, Maintain Good Posture - Good posture is one of the few body language gestures that you can maintain when you're sitting or standing. This one is going to be particularly useful during interviews or business negotiations. Maintaining good posture even when you're sitting down conveys a sense of professionalism, and it makes you look authoritative on the subject to anyone who's listening to you speak. It is also an important gesture to maintain when you're communicating since it lets your audience know that you're completely engaged and focused on the message that you're delivering.
- Maintain Open Posture - Maintaining an open posture is another body language gesture that can be done both while you're sitting and standing up. Yet, forgetting to maintain an open posture when in the seated position is a mistake that often gets made by most, especially during a boardroom discussion. A speaker that keeps their hands clasped together on the table or puts their arms in the "locked" position closes themselves off to the audience,

creating a physical barrier that prevents them from appearing open and honest.

- Maintaining the Right Amount of Gestures - Sitting down and being too stiff when you're speaking is not going to convince anyone, no matter how much your ideas make sense. You look far too rigid when you forget to gesture naturally, so even when you're sitting down, don't forget to gesture when you're trying to emphasize a point, just like what you would do when you're standing. Use your arms and your hands at the right moments during your speech to really make your audience sit up and say "Wow! That was brilliant!".

Virtual Persuasion

What about if you were speaking to your audience virtually, though? Like what those who work as customer service or telemarketers would need to do? With the many options, technology has afforded us with today, even business conferences and client meetings could take place over the phone or through video conferencing. To be persuasive in a virtual setting is going to be even more challenging than trying to do it face-to-face since your audience can't exactly see you and gauge your responses accurately enough. However, it is still possible to pull off the art of persuasion, even when you're doing it virtually, by relying on the following techniques to get it done:

- Smile - Smiling, even when it's being done over the phone, makes you sound much friendlier and warmer, and even if the person on the other end of the line can't see you, they can certainly pick up on the verbal cues in your voice. When you speak with a smile, your vocal cords are pulled in such a way that it makes your voice automatically sound more pleasant, cheerful and upbeat. Try this simple exercise of saying "Hello, how can I help you today?" and say it once with a smile, and once without. Notice the difference in your voice when you do? That's what the receiver is going to be hearing on the other end of the line.

- Move Around and Stand Up - Whenever possible, aim to move around and stand up when you're talking over the phone or virtually. The receiver may not be able to see you, but they can certainly hear the expressiveness in your voice when you're speaking to them. You must be just as involved and engaged in the conversation with the same enthusiasm you would have if they were standing right in front of you.

- Rely Heavily on Your Vocals - Since the visual clues which are so vital to the communication and persuasion process are going to be heavily absent during virtual conversations, your vocals need to now pick up the pace. Your voice is the only thing right now convincing your receiver, and you need to put as much gusto, passion, and enthusiasm into your voice as you can manage.

Effective Communication for Couples

Excellent communication is a significant element of all affairs and is an important ingredient of any good relationship. Every affair has difficulties; however, good communication approaches might make it simple to handle disagreement and make a stronger relationship. People understand how vital interaction is, bar not what communication is and how people may apply excellent communication in their affairs. People regularly perplex communication for speaking or making discussion, and this is the reason why several of these persons are so unproductive when it comes to how to interact effectively. Communication in an affair, at its best, is about linking and applying your oral, printed, and physical abilities to accomplish your partner's desires. It is not concerning making tiny talk. It concerns understanding your partner's position; giving support and permitting your spouse to know that you are his or her admirer.

Before you struggle on developing your communication in an affair, you require understanding that not everybody has the similar communication inclinations. Several persons like to speak some desire touch while other people are visual or react better to present giving than an external conversation of thoughts. Everyone is inimitable and reacts to different motivations in different ways, and efficient interaction with your spouse shall come from accepting this. Your spouse might be telling you accurately what they require, however you have to be aware of how they express this message to you. If there is a lack of communication, you shall miss the chance to develop trust and confidence, and you shall both feel aggravated in the affair.

Be available in your affair

To develop communication in affairs and accurately realize what your spouse is communicating to you, be present. Set time away and give yourself a hundred per cent to converse with your spouse. He or she must truly feel that they have your undivided concentration and that he or she is your main concern. It is intricate to pay attention and be available, conscious, and attentive when you are annoyed and worried or are struggling with issues that need time far from your bond. This is a component of life; however, it is vital to understand that it is not a justification for abandoning communication in an affair. Keep in mind that closeness, love, and dependence are developed when matters are complicated, not when they are simple. If we surrender at each mark of struggle, we could never develop and progress. Grab these chances to discover how to deal with disagreement and pressure in a healthy way and observe as you develop and thrive with your spouse.

Defy letting an easy conversation regarding what is happening currently decentralize into a repeat of every mistake that has ever occurred between you and your spouse. This is the reverse of caring and efficient communication in an affair. Pause and memorize why you are in the relationship and recall that your objective, the result that you cherish, is to reinforce your relationship, create intimacy, and find out how to talk better. How to converse effectively is more than expressing the correct feelings. You must also be attentive to body language. Someone might give all the caring and kind words in the world to your spouse, however, if your hands are folded on your upper body and you have a frown on your face, your spouse is unlikely to react positively. How to converse in an association implies paying attention, caring, and supporting your entire effort. Bend toward your spouse, keep your look calm and open, and tap him or her in a temperate manner. Prove to him or her through all your terms, deeds and expressions that you are his or her lover even if you are in disagreement.

Be straightforward
Retreating from disagreement seems dishonestly secure and calm, however, it is no alternative for trust in an affair, and it shall never assist you to discover how to communicate effectively. Moving away from a fight is a momentary method of dealing with a constant communication concern and must be done for achieving a short cooling-down time. When you differ with your spouse, you must be capable of trusting that what you speak shall be heard and appreciated, and so does

your spouse.

When you or your spouse are unenthusiastic to disagreement, you might get yourselves concealing your feelings to satisfy each other and evade troubles. This momentary mediation band-aid spins a collaborative affair into a one-way lane, and that is not a good result. The cheerfulness and closeness you used to have shall progressively wear away, and it shall take the association with it. On the other hand, instead of paying no attention to matters, it is vital that you both find out how to converse effectively to one another.

Effective communication for seduction
The work of seducing is a delicate and alluring entertainment, which entails using the correct quantity of display or camouflage, magnificent or revealing vaguely, stating something, but not revealing a lot. This discontinuous between an individual and the other plays a huge role in seductive communication in which the purpose to lessen the interpersonal space with hopes to enhance closeness is strongly tangled with the desire to save one's pride in case of dismissal. It also regards the preference of

communicative deeds, which is deliberately allusive: to be competent, it must entail giving a clue of what is on display without illuminating too much. Simplicity and referential data are surely not the idiosyncratic aspects of seductive interaction; in fact, what appears to matter most is how the match is played, instead of the components of the match itself.

For this uniqueness, seductive contact stands out in its personal right as a tip of examination in communicative manners. Mainly it makes it probable to scrutinize the connections between diverse structures of expression and to explain some tactic of obliquity and camouflage skill, which are defined as miscommunication types.

Communication in marriage

Good marriage flourishes on the free exchange of feeling, wishes, and ideas. In addition, interaction is one of the most significant features of an enjoyable marriage. Marriages experiences tough times, which might alter the manner spouses, converse with each other. Several partners grow bad behaviour and create unhelpful patterns when matters are not working well. Excellent communication is the basis of a happy marriage. Several marriages can be saved if partners improved the manner, they talk to each other. It is frequently the simplest terrible behaviour that gets partners into difficulty. When a marriage falls on a bumpy track, unconstructiveness develops. Troubles shoot up as both partners duplicate their fault repeatedly.

Shouting at your partner
If you feel annoyed, you possibly begin raising your tone. Rage creates anxiety. As nervousness develops, you search for means of letting it go or saying it. Shouting at your partner becomes an immediate and easy choice, although it frequently causes more difficulty than help. It might be excellent to let loose your anxiety on your partner when he or she upset you, however, the sense of fulfilment is regularly transitory what you speak in your irritated condition is expected to add firewood to the bonfire.
Shouting unleashes many strong, unenthusiastic feelings. Regardless of the message, you are attempting to converse at that point, the feeling shall be the focal point.

It is not that you may not express several strong feelings when you talk. However, shouting goes past the contour. It makes the point for an exchange of intense sentiments rather than unmistakably communicated expressions. Even if your feeling is the information you want to share, an entirely sentimental exchange might easily change into a fatiguing, negative routine. At some position, feelings require to outbreak in a manner that lets you go past them, not stimulate them.

Allow your expressions to speak
If you might keep your feelings in check, your point might really go through. This does not imply you must attempt shoving your feelings out of the track. They might be a vital element of your circumstances. However, remember the entire purpose of communicating is to be unmistakably understood. To enable that, your path of communication should follow two ways. Extreme sentiment meddles with that. Take time by yourself to assist you to drive the wave of emotions and allow them to stay separately.

Another alternative is to take a swift work

outbreak before you carry on the discussion. Exercise is a wonderful pressure reducer and it might easily divert you from your powerful feelings. It is hard to concentrate on your plight if you are almost out of breath. You might as well find it accommodating to note down the issues that you desire to state so you take care to convey your point noticeably. It is good to take time discussing a subject that makes you emotional. You shall solve the crisis effortlessly if you might keep your partner on your side **rather than pushing him or her away.**

   Avoid cutthroat mind-set
You might have to be competitive in the game in some regions of your days, but your matrimony is not a completion. When one individual is constantly the conqueror, both partners lose. When you see yourself making a case in your brain with supporting evidence for every difference, you might triumph the disagreement each time. Nevertheless, you might do more to drain and dishearten your partner than something else.

The desire to succeed

An individual with emotional doubts might overcompensate by attempting to look greater than his or her partner attempts. If he or she stays successful, they feel better and more positive. They might have difficulty being susceptible, even with their partner. To do so could reveal their doubts. This could conflict with their trust that they are victorious. Does your partner exhaust of your success in dancing and you require to always having the final say? Perhaps they just desire you to go down. They are maybe better off to be next to you when you prove fault. You might not be used to your partner showing kindness toward you. when you married a good individual, you have nothing to worry about and everything to be happy. You do not have to be successful to feel happy.

Avoid being self-centred

Have you constantly stopped paying attention to the talk going on in your brain? In most cases, it is centred on what you appear, how you muddled, and what you have on your timetable.

Logically, this talk is somewhat unfair because it is from your perception. Nevertheless, how about the talk that refers to your partner? Is it concerning how much enjoyment you shall have, what you anticipate from your lover, and what type of disposition you are experiencing?

Accept your partner's opinion

Kindness and understanding behaviours might go a long way toward fostering a good marriage. Instead of speculating if they shall ever fill the dishwasher correctly, do something you understand your partner shall value. When you maintain a model of being kind and considerate toward your partner, they will ultimately speak or do something as a reaction. They may hood their comments, as they do not recognize if this trend shall continue. They might be patient to see if this kindness is a publicity stunt or a set of fresh, positive routines. When they notice that you are real and constant with your hard work over time, your point shall be understandable. Allow those self-centred feelings pass by and continue doing adoring things for your partner. Additionally, you might not feel adoring at first if you do this kind of work. If your spouse does not speak something, you might question why you are struggling at all. The more you try with bigheartedness, the more you shall unsurprisingly feel kind and adoring toward your partner.

Adjust Communication errors by altering behaviour

It takes several practices to alter mature marriage communication faults. It is remarkable how the energy between partners might adjust so much with a few alterations. When you know how it all suits together, you might make genuine growth in your marriage.

Avoiding redundancy in your marriage
When someone is about to become redundant,
his or her money is doubtless his or her main
worry. However, redundancy might bring
other troubles in its wake, as well. Both
subjective proof and serious arithmetical
studies prove that redundancy might put your
relationship under great pressure. It might be
that the relationship has been conflicting for a
while, and all joblessness does is argument the
extrication. However, joblessness may even
make troubles in marriages that appeared
joyful and established before.

No one likes having to give redundancy notes.
Definitely, anybody who has had to do it shall
tell you it is the nastiest elements of their work.
On the other hand, not everybody shall be
dejected regarding his or her redundancy.
Several people shall have energetically
pursued it to seek a different job, business, or
way of life. However, it is those moments
when you are handing out joblessness to those
who are not expecting it and do not desire it
who are the hardest to handle.
Redundancy may be categorized as a distress
in spite of how much information someone is

given. When we reflect on the matters that assist us to be safe in life, our jobs are indeed one of them. Losing a career, for whatever cause, might come as distress even when you understood it was going to happen. It is a huge alteration and as career people, we do not take alterations well. There are changes that occur out of the alteration but first you must accept the feelings of refusal, sorrow, nervousness, fright, and concern, loss of self-worth and loss of your senses as you doubtless connected your sense of worth to your work.

For a partner, dealing with your treasured one's alteration in conditions may be traumatic in all types of ways. Your capability to assist them to deal with the redundancy stage might have a crucial influence on how your spouse deals with the change and moves on with life. Away from assisting your spouse through this stage, you shall have the extra weight of struggling with your worry and, maybe, those of your kids. Partners shall frequently experience the suffering of joblessness as much as the hunt for employment. A lot of the subsequent recommendation might seem to be common sense; several of it might seem hard to put into practice. However, even for the trickiest troubles, there is relieve to be achieved by simply being alert that they might happen; and from being capable of reassuring yourself that, your responses to the feeling are shared by the several other persons who have had to experience joblessness.

How redundancy terrorize your relationship
Financial troubles are one of the major causes of marriage collapse after joblessness. Loss of wages can put the children home in danger if you cannot maintain the finance expenditure. Too many partners, the house they acquired together might seem like a substantial personification of the marriage. When the house it goes and they are required to start fresh living planning, the relationship itself frequently disintegrates, as well.

If one spouse is made superfluous whereas the other is still working, it forms an unhealthy monetary reliance and an inequity of power in the marriage. The dependence might soon make itself evident in other means as one spouse, tries to force his or her wish on the other partner with the sense of privilege that roots from being the household's lone wage earner. Ironically, although extreme hours toiled by one spouse are one of the major reasons for separation in the world nowadays, the reverse, the compulsory joblessness that may follow idleness, might also be tremendously negative to a marriage. The complete physical issue of being in the house more frequently, and sharing time together, implies that there are chances for you both getting in one another's skin. One of the partners might become short-tempered, and the marriage might start to collapse.

Dealing with the problem redundancy brings in your relationship

Apart from getting fresh work, and therefore solving the trouble, the best method to deal with the stress that redundancy puts forth on your marriage with your spouse is purely to be conscious of it. If you are aware of the situations that might result in joblessness, and see yourself going into one of them, you might hold down yourself and desist from doing or speaking something insensible, which you may later feel sorry. You may also speak about the difficulty openly with your spouse and admit that redundancy brings trouble to your relationship.

Relationship Counselling

When you sense that your relationship is starting to fall apart, seeing a marriage psychotherapist might assist. There are some marriage therapy charities all over the world that give their services free or for a little cost. Though every marriage is exceptional, the occurrence of a joblessness causing stress in a relationship is one that the counsellors shall surely have experienced before. There is no enchantment stick for erasing away marriage predicament. However, most partners depart counselling perceiving that they have achieved something from the counsellor, even if it is superior insight into the state of the troubles they encounter.

Effective Communication for Friends

You've read this in every advice column, and it isn't really a secret — communication is the key of any successful, rewarding and gratifying relationship. I know it sounds similar to "just be yourself." But how does one really do that? It sounds amazing in theory and social media posters. However, how can it be applied in our practical, everyday life? Here are some practical and highly actionable tips and insights to increase your communication skills when it comes to personal relationships.

1. Avoid Communicating When Under High Stress

In high-stress situations, we often say or do things we regret. Happens all the time, right? There is also a tendency to take everything that a person says personally. Our judgment becomes skewed, and we lose our sense of logic. Instead, focus on returning to a calm state of mind before addressing the issue or concern. You'll think more and speak more coherently.

You won't end up saying things you'll regret or that will further aggravate the problem. When you are in a calm and relaxed state of mind, you'll know whether to respond to the situation or remain silent. Use stalling techniques. Offer yourself some time to think and go over the issue. Pause for a while and collect your thoughts. Pausing is better than rushing into a response only to say the wrong things. The golden rule of communication within personal relationships is to avoid saying anything under stress and duress. Wait to calm down and then make your points in a coherent and logical manner.

Of course, it is easier said than done because strong emotions are involved. However, each time you find yourself getting stressed or angry, just keep a technique ready to gain more calmness. For example, when things get heated up and stressed, some people just like going out and walking for a few minutes before getting back to the discussion. They come back calmer and less stressed.

Even in the middle of a heated argument or discussion, don't lose your balance. Speak coherently, keep an even tone and make eye contact with the person you are addressing. Your body language should be relaxed, unperturbed and open. Don't reveal any signs of nervousness, anxiety or stress through your body language. When you notice that things are getting emotionally intense, swing into action to bring down the level of emotional intensity! Bring down stress, manage your feelings and act appropriately.

Our body automatically gives out signals when we feel stressed and anxious. Your muscles will feel tighter. The hands will slowly clench. Your breathing becomes shallower. These are all physical symptoms of stress. Take a deep breath and calm down. If you are not up for it, postpone the conversation or take a short break before getting back to it.

Sensory experiences are one of the best ways to kill momentary stress. Through sensory experiences including sound, smell, sight, taste, and movement, you can beat stress. For instance, pop a candy in your mouth and notice how it tastes. How about taking a few deep breaths? Or visualizing a happy memory! These are sensory-rich experiences that can help reduce your stress. Every person has a different response to sensory inputs. Identify things that relax and soothe you.

2. Be Assertive

Being assertive doesn't mean you fight with your loved ones on every issue that comes up. It simply means standing up for yourself and not let people walk all over you. Being assertive in personal relationships helps you set boundaries and prevents people from taking you for granted. It also paves the way for clear communication, decision-making and increasing your self-esteem.

Assertive people express their thoughts in an honest, confident and open manner. They stand up for themselves and respect others around them. Being assertive should not be mistaken for being hostile, demanding, dogmatic or aggressive. It is about understanding the other person and being understood without focusing on winning the argument. An assertive communicator will always attempt to come up with a middle way rather than being obsessed with winning an argument or forcing their opinion on the other person.

How does one develop greater assertiveness to communicate effectively in personal relationships? Value yourself and your views/opinion. Understand that they are as important as the other person's. Identify your needs and wants and learn to express them without trampling on other people's rights. Learn to express even negative thoughts in a positive way. Stay respectful even when you are involved in an ugly feud with a person. This gets people to listen to you and take your words seriously. Being disrespectful takes away from your credibility, while also making people switch off after a while!

One of the most important things for being an assertive communicator is to know your limits and to say no when you mean no. Don't let people take advantage of you. When you aren't up for something, politely, firmly and respectfully say no. Look for solutions where everyone will feel happy with the outcome. Demonstrate an empathetic assertion in personal relationships, where you acknowledge the other person's feelings but also express yours freely and clearly. For example, "I understand that you've been working very hard, but I also want you to make …. for us." Then there's escalating assertion, which can be used when your initial attempts to be assertive are not successfully met. For instance, "If you don't stick to what we've mutually agreed about your addiction and abusive ways, I will be forced to consider separation/divorce." This is different from threatening a person. You are merely stating the consequences if your rights or needs are overlooked.

I know some people aren't naturally assertive or don't have a confident personality. It can be developed with practice. Start by practicing in lower risk scenarios to build up the confidence and skills for high-risk situations. Practice assertiveness techniques on people whom you trust and who are capable of giving you honest feedback.

3. Focus on Collaborative Communication

One of the most significant problems of communication in personal relationships during modern times is a misconception where the objective of communication is concerned. Most view it as a battle or debate between two parties, when in fact, the idea is to cooperate and collaborate and not compete. If either partner goes into the conversation without an accurate reality perception. Both parties don't have access to identifying what the reality is. The purpose of communication is, therefore, determining what the real situation is. Communication involves collaborating as both the parties share their feelings, perception, ideas, and thoughts to arrive at a correct understanding of what happened.

While approaching a conversation with your partner, disarm. This simply means give up your obsession to be right or win the argument. This isn't a war that has to be won. I any damage is done you both lose. Again, on the other side, this doesn't mean you have to compromise or give in to everything he or she says. You obviously have the right to feel the emotions you feel. However, all the same, think that your partner may have something to say worth hearing or considering. Stop treating every conversation as a battleground where you have to prove you are right all the time. There is no real victory in these situations.

4. Identify the Other Person's Communication Style and Your Own

Recognizing your and the other person's communication style is one of the best ways to communicate more effectively with them while also eliminating instances of misunderstanding and conflict. Here are some primary communication styles that can be identified and built upon to accomplish more harmonious and fulfilling interactions.

Assertive communicators. These are people who possess a high sense of self-esteem, self-assuredness, and self-confidence. This is known to be the healthiest communication style that seeks to work out a middle way between being too passive or aggressive while also staying away from manipulation games. Assertive people realize their limits and don't want to be pushed around by people who want to use them to get things done. All the same, they won't violate other people's emotions or rights to fulfill their purpose. The assertive communicator style is win-win because confident communicators come up with solutions that are beneficial for everyone involved, compared to merely thinking about their own needs.

Typical characteristics of an assertive communicator — they accomplish goals without hurting others; they protect their own rights while also being respectful of other people's rights. They are more socially and emotionally expressive. Assertive communicators make their own choices and accept responsibility for these choices.

Their typical nonverbal behavior includes medium pitch, volume, and speed of speech. Their posture is open, relaxed, and symmetrical. They stand tall, and there are barely any signs of fidgeting or nervousness. Their gestures are open, expansive and rounded. Assertive people typically make good eye contact and maintain a spatial position that conveys they are respectful of others and in control.

Typical things they say include, "Please would you lower the volume? I am finding it tough to focus on my work" or "I am sorry I won't be able to help with your homework because I have an appointment scheduled with my physician." Try and be an assertive communicator if you want to be effective.

Aggressive communicators. This style is all about winning — unfortunately at other people's expense. Aggressive communicators act like their needs are supreme, and nothing or no one else matters. They behave like they are born with greater rights, and have a bigger say in things than others around them. Predictably, this isn't an effective communication style. Since aggressive communicators focus excessively on the delivery of their message, the content is invariably lost.

Their nonverbal behavior includes loud volume, bigger and more expansive posture than other people, fast and jerky facial expressions and a spatial position that invades other people's space or tries to stand upon other people. Typical language used by them includes "you are insane" or "this has to be done in my way" or "you make me mad." Blaming, taunting, name-calling, insulating, sarcasm and threatening are all characteristics of an aggressive communicator.

Passive-aggressive communicators. These communicators appear passive on the outside but are actually playing out their anger 'behind the scenes.' These people generally feel powerless and are mostly resentful. They subtly undermine targets of their resentment, often even at the cost of sabotaging themselves. Passive aggressive will typically say things like "why don't you move ahead and do this. My ideas aren't of any value anyway" or "you always know more than others anyway." There is a hint of sarcasm in what they say.

Their body language involves speaking in a sugar sweet voice, maintaining an asymmetrical posture, jerky and quick gestures and facial expressions that appear sweet and innocent. The passive aggressive spatial position involves standing too close. At times, even touching other people while pretending to be friendly, warm and affable!

Submissive communicators. Submissive communicators are about pleasing people and avoiding confrontation at any cost. They will bend backward to please other people often at the cost of their own wants and needs. Typically, submissive communicators place other people's needs before theirs. They believe their needs aren't as crucial as people around them. This leads to disillusionment and frustration. Typical language used by them includes, "Oh! It's really nothing, don't worry" or "Oh! Its fine, I really don't want it any longer" or "You pick, anything is alright with me."

Manipulative communicator. Manipulative communicators are shrewd, scheming and calculating. They prey upon other people's feelings and emotions to serve their purpose. Manipulative communicators possess the ability to influence and control people for their own benefit. The words they speak almost always have underlying or hidden messages, which their victims are unaware of.

Their typical verbiage includes, "you are so fortunate to enjoy these delicious chocolates. I wish I were lucky enough to have them too. I can't afford such pricey chocolates" or "I didn't have time to purchase anything, so I had no option but to wear this attire. I am crossing my fingers that I don't look too bad in it." Their voice is patronizing, often bordering on envious, high-pitched and ingratiating, while facial expressions are typically "hangdog."

5. Use "I" Statements

Of course, you want to express your feelings, desires, and needs. It is an important part of being an assertive communicator. You can express your needs, desires, and feelings without attributing blame to the other person. This is one of the biggest secrets of communicating effectively in personal relationships. You can communicate what you want to say without offending the other person by using "I" statements instead of "You" statements.

By using "I" instead of "You", you take responsibility for your actions rather than passing on the blame to another person. It is direct, non-accusatory and honest. It emphasizes the person's behavior and it's after effects. "I" statements comprise talk about the other person's behavior, your feelings, and consequences. Typically, it is like "I feel…….when…….because………. " Or "even I feel…….when you……….and would prefer……….."

Be specific when you are referring to another person's behavior, refer to a current or recent incident instead of generalizing it. Ensure you own your feelings, and that you accept responsibility for your feelings rather than accusing others. No one can make you feel something. Keep your body language and tone calm, relaxed and open. Avoid making these statements in a more passive-aggressive or sarcastic manner. It won't come across as genuine.

Some example of accusatory "you" statements and "I" statements are as follows. While blaming "you statements" state something like, "you are working late again, just like always." The same statement can be converted into an "I" statement by saying something like, "I feel frustrated when you work late because it doesn't allow me to spend more time with you." Similarly, instead of saying "you don't love me anymore", try saying something like, "I feel lonely when you stop calling me for long periods. Can we work something out so I don't feel like this anymore?"

See what we are doing here? We are accepting responsibility for our feelings instead of blaming or accusing the other person. You are telling the other person that you are experiencing a particular feeling rather than them being responsible for it. You are expressing your desire without pointing the finger at the other person, which works wonders.

6. Make Small Talk

Yes I know it's your partner of 20 years, a family member or a close person we are talking about here and not a stranger you've just met at a party. However, if experts are to go by, small talk about seemingly insignificant details have a more substantial impact on your emotional ties than so-called, profound or deep emotional conversations. Psychoanalyst Harry Stack Sullivan created an approach that he referred to as "detailed inquiry", where he recommended therapists to accumulate as much information about a client's life as possible to find clues about his or her personality.

Research conducted by John Gottman and Janice Driver researched this suggestion with a group of married folks and discovered that boring or mundane details or the seemingly trivial moments which are a part of a couple's everyday life have a greater bearing on a relationship's health than emotionally serious and so-called meaningful conversations. This makes making small talk with your partner an excellent idea!

Similarly, research published in Psychological Science reveals that we connect better with others when we are able to talk about everyday experiences. Say, for instance, you are attempting to repair a ruptured relationship or marriage, start with the children. Speak about positive memories and amusing/cute incidents related to your children. Avoid referring to moments of conflict or discord. Find shared memories and moments — this can be one of the most effective solutions when it is about a child you both adore.

7. Listen, Listen, Listen

This is all the more critical when it comes to our personal relationships. Since we are so used to having the person around us, many times, we just take what they are saying for granted and don't practice active listening. Knowing that what you are saying is being keenly heard is one of the best feelings in the world. It brings about a sense of connection between people.

One way to sharpen your listening skills is to practice active listening. You are not just nodding your head and offering verbal acknowledgments, but you are also comprehending what is being said. Understanding can be conveyed through everything from your smile to a word or a phrase, to whatever unique nonverbal cues you use to communicate you are listening to the other person. Active listening also comprises interrupting the other person while he or she is speaking or asking for clarifications (which reveal you have been listening to the other person).

Disagreements also signify active listening. But how can you disagree with a person if you haven't heard what he or she is speaking about? If you are interrupting the person to seek permission, say something like, "sorry for interrupting you but can I ask you something?" This is a reasonable request if you want to ask something when the person hasn't finished speaking yet. If you're going to disagree with the person, wait until they've made all their points or finished speaking.

They may have something that you may agree with at the end of their talk, so hold on until the end to disagree. If you feel that they haven't described something accurately, seek more clarification rather than downright accusing them of manipulation, lies or deceit. You may gain greater clarity by asking them more questions.

Non-Violent Communication

Things are bound to flare up in your relationships. There will be times when things become so thick people cannot see eye to eye, and this is when nonviolent communication (NVC) will come into play.

NVC prevents conflicts from taking place by helping to establish a foundation of respect and trust when people communicate. The beauty of NVC is that even at the point when you feel most angry and ready to flare up and when your initial response will be overboard because you were angry, NVC causes you to act in a trusting and respectful manner, without a hint of passive aggression that typically causes resentment and distrust.

By definition, NVC is a communication framework designed to reduce conflict and tension among the people. It provides us with a lens that gives us an entirely different perspective of the world. It also changes how people express themselves to others, connect and communicate with others, and how they empathize with them. Essentially, NVC enables you to create a better, higher quality connection so that people may enjoy being in a relationship that has mutually beneficial outcomes.

Below are a few of the features of an NVC:
 1. Peaceful Resolution of Conflicts
Conflicts are a normal part of interacting and relating with other people, but the important thing is to resolve them peacefully and productively, and this process requires some considerable time, support, and lots of practice. Peaceful conflict resolution engages both parties and has them working together to de-escalate, process, and resolve a conflict situation.
In this case, rather than confronting each other or burying the conflict as a whole, feuding persons are encouraged to demonstrate courage by opening up to each other regarding the conflict and how it affected them. They are also asked to show compassion to each other's side of the story, empathizing with the other party's experiences or interpretation of the events. Thirdly, the parties are asked to work together, in collaboration, to process the conflict and to come up with a resolution plan.

Here are the guidelines that help to chatter the way as you work towards resolving your c0nflict in a peaceful, healthy, and kind way, even in the circumstances that are very tense: Remain calm: remember that you control your emotions and not the other way. You must be able to manage your anger emotions before you can help another person manage his. Whichever method you use, from breathing deeply to others you may have up your sleeve, the idea here is to keep your emotions under wraps long enough to allow a negotiation There are no winners: sometimes, the conflict will revolve around a ridiculous issue of little or no consequence. For example, don't get caught up in conflict regarding a football match that happened or even one that is going to happen. Although fans can be very passionate, the players determine which team wins and which ones lose by their playing in the field. As fans, you have to sit back and watch. Don't lose your peace over things you have no control over, especially those that do not require your participation. Also, do not fear to submit to another's opinions regarding issues like these because they do not influence your life in the first place.

Give audience to the other party: If someone is making you part of an uncomfortable conversation, give them the opportunity to speak as much as they need to. Acting disinterested or interrupting them while they talk will not work in your favor; it will only aggravate the situation. Remember that at the time, the person is not rational, and he can pull you in that direction. Therefore, give him time to get everything off his system and eventually, things will calm down.

Do not engage in verbal insults: when resolving a conflict, be watchful of your tone and the words you use. Avoid abusive or angry words; let your inner voice do the work. Audibly speaking profanity, screaming, and using hateful language only escalates the conflict.

Maintain a safe and comfortable distance: If you fear that the situation could quickly deteriorate and turn physical, keep a safe distance from the other person. This will keep the person from attacking you or from interpreting your physical moves as offensive postures. Therefore, keep your distance and do not give room for the other person to feel threatened.

Overall, when you want to resolve a conflict peacefully, seek higher ground. Ask yourself, "Is it better to be right or happy?"

2. Reconciliation after a Conflict

After a conflict, reconciliation allows parties to return to working together to build the society and to achieve the shared goals. Parties must begin to move past their divided opinions into a shared future. Reconciliation is meant to restore the relationship between people to allow for future engagements and collaborations. Unfortunately, reconciliation can be quite difficult, especially because there are so many setbacks and failures involved, depending on the depth of the conflict. However, the only real failure would be if the parties involved did not consider reconciliation.

There is no definite systematic process that parties can follow to resolve a conflict; each situation demands a unique approach. However, there are some lessons you could carry away to help you resolve the conflicts in your life:

Reconciliation is both the process and the destination.

Reconciliation cannot be done in haste because it takes time to address the underlying issues such as anger, pain, frustration, and others. Reconciliation processes should not be judged as either successes or failures because each process will have its micro wins and successes Reconciliation is done in several stages, and parties should expect relapses too.

Mutual interests can be very effective in facilitating reconciliation between feuding parties.

With the understanding that reconciliation does not involve specific steps, parties should, however, ensure that both sides are heard. Parties must also be ready to abandon their old beliefs.

3. Secrets of Mediating Knowledge

There will be situations where the only thing feuding parties can agree on is that they need the help of a mediator. The mediator ought to be a neutral party, whose role is not to judge and declare the winner and the loser. His goal is to help the parties come to an understanding.

Mediation takes place in two stages. The first stage is the joint session. Mediation begins by holding a meeting that lets the mediator in the prevailing situation. The parties present their facts, and each side indicates what its ideal resolution of the situation would be. The mediator also needs to have all the information regarding what started the conflict and where it has gotten to as at now.

The second stage is the caucus stage, and in this one, the mediator is obliged to hold separate sessions with each party. The details of the meeting should be highly confidential but for the statements that the first party would want to be repeated to the second party. The mediator then collects each side's interests, including information about the concerns and needs that the dispute is affecting.

Once the second stage is done, the mediator then begins moving from one party to another, collecting proposals and suggestions that the parties believe will satisfy their interests equally. Ultimately, a solution is reached. Sometimes, it will be a one-sided victory while other times, it will end in a 'win-win' situation.

4. Making Bad Thoughts Disappear

When bad thoughts plague your mind, closing your eyes as tightly as you can do not shut them out. The thought or the feeling keeps popping up, over and over. The thoughts could be of a disturbing story you heard on the news, nagging self-doubt, or thoughts of your relationship that went sour. All these thoughts make you miserable and cause you to feel imprisoned by your cruel mind.

Some people believe in the divine, and will invoke the power of their deities to drive the negative thoughts away, while the second group believes that nothing can be done about it. They believe that these thoughts have to come up and that blocking them out is only a waste of time. The good news is that you can totally block out unproductive thoughts, but only when armed with the right strategies. One fact you must remember is that blocking out the negative thoughts is an effort in futility because one way or another, the thoughts rebound. However, it is possible to block out the negative thoughts and not have any rebounds; you only need to remember two things.

The first is that blocking the thought is difficult, but just because it is difficult does not mean that you need to think about it. Your brain is not out to get you with the negativities. Stop thinking about the difficulty of letting the thoughts go because it is this thinking that gives the thought more meaning and importance, making it even more challenging to get rid of.

The second step is to know how to handle negative thought when it shows up. The solution is to plan, in advance, what to do when the thought comes to mind. Some opt to ignore it while others choose to replace the negative thought with some positive ones.

5. Using Positive Language

Language is quite a powerful tool, and the manner in which you express yourself affects how it is received, whether positively or negatively. Positive language is so effective it is used to convey even bad news. It also elicits cooperation and reception, unlike negative language that arouses confrontation and argument. In your daily communication, positive language helps to project a positive, helpful image while negative language projects a destructive image.

You must have come across a naysayer in the course of your life. A naysayer is a person who criticizes ideas, always having an opinion about why an idea won't work. Sometimes, the naysayer won't even have a negative attitude, he or she will just speak using words or a tone that implies negativity. If you have been around someone like that, you know just how annoying and mentally fatiguing a person like that can be.

Since naysayers get creative by the day, here is how you identify negative language: it carries the message that you cannot do something, it subtly blames you, it does not mention or stress the positive consequences, and it includes words like can't, unable to, won't, and other words that let the listener or the reader know what cannot be done.

Positive language, on the other hand, will tell you what can be done, it will sound encouraging or helpful than bureaucratic, offer suggestions of possible alternatives and it stresses the positive actions or consequences that the reader or listener should expect. You certainly would want to lean towards positive language so that you can be a fountain of hope and positivity for others. Take up positive language and positive thinking, and replace all your negative statements with positive ones.

6. Being Honest

Honesty is one of the simplest values to practice, yet it can take you to heights you never imagined. It can also make you so fulfilled, happy, and successful better than any other virtue. Trust honesty to rip through deceit and lies. As a noble human being, honesty should be one of the foundational pillars of your core principles and values in life.

By definition, honesty is not just about telling the truth; it also is about you being real with yourself and with others about who you are on the inside, what you like, and what is most important to you, if you are going to lead an authentic life. Honesty empowers you and causes you to be more open so that you have consistency in your delivery of facts. It also sharpens your focus and perception, allowing you to see the things around you with greater clarity.

If you are not honest, you certainly are lying or being deceitful. Lying is terrible, whether you are deceiving yourself or others. Whenever you lie, you fool yourself into believing the things you're saying. You also begin to dig a ditch of hypocrisy that only gets bigger with time. A liar confuses himself and others around him, losing all credibility, and possibly putting himself in harm's way.

Deception gets even more serious when you deceive yourself. It all begins with you messing around with the concepts of right and wrong, morality, and the concepts of desires and dreams. You will find yourself lying to be able to do something you very well know is wrong. When you do this once and succeed, nothing will stop the chain of lies that follows. You will lie to have your way, to misrepresent your shortcomings, or to have the upper hand unjustly. Lies set you on the path to crime.

If you want to be a law-abiding, honest citizen, then honesty is the way to go. It will build your faith, empower your will, and increase your confidence. It will also ensure that you present your authentic self to others, and you will attract only those who want to be in your life. You will not have to live your life pretending or feigning an attitude or putting up a front as people do for their fake friends. Your life will be peaceful, and you will enjoy every bit of it.

7. Creating Feelings

One of the greatest discoveries of my life has been that my feelings are the product of the thoughts I have been having all day. If your thoughts focus on the positive side of life and on bright, happy things, you are bound to feel happy about yourself. This goes to show that if you master your thoughts throughout the day, you will have mastered your feelings.

More than anything, you want to have a happy life by being happy with who you are and accepting others for who they are. Positive feelings cause you to feel good, energetic, determined, and able to take action to pursue and achieve what you want. They improve your relationship with others and make you likable.

To develop positive feelings, often think about the positive effects the feelings will bring to your life and the immense changes that could come from it. Do not allow your mind to engage in negative thoughts and feelings. When you wake up, before you do anything else, smile and declare to yourself, "I will have a wonderful day today!" As you go about your day, look back to the times when you were happy and visualize the joys you will be having in the days to come, also. If something makes you angry, wait a while before you react, see if it is worth your attention. Some things are minor and only need to be ignored. To remain positive, whenever you meet people you don't like, try to show them some positivity. It doesn't mean that you suddenly become friends; it only helps to keep you from having negative thoughts. Inspirational quotes, some funny comedies, and some music will also help keep up the positivity. Some people even take up meditation to help them get rid of the thoughts they don't want. As you get into bed at the end of the day, make another declaration and say, "I will have an awesome day tomorrow!"

Take up any other habit that makes you feel happy, so long as it does not hurt or infringe on the happiness of other people.

8. Making and Receiving Good Praise

When it comes to motivating the people around you, or when someone wants to motivate you offering praise and recognition can have quite a positive effect. We all feel good when others praise us. This kind of recognition brings up feelings of pride, pressure, and raises a person's self-esteem. This is because praise releases a burst of dopamine, the feel-good hormone that controls pleasure and reward centers in the brain. The result is a good feeling that could change the trajectory of a person's life, change his self-image or at the very least, brighten his day. On the other hand, the wrong praise, delivered at the wrong time, in the wrong company can be quite devastating. It can crush a man, crush his spirit, and crush his esteem. For this reason, when thinking about offering praise to someone, there are key factors you need to consider.

The first is that at the very least, your praise should have the name of the person you are recognizing, mention the specific thing you are praising him or her for, and it should be sincere. Mentioning a name conveys respect and special recognition. Mentioning the specifics makes the praise sound more sincere as opposed to a vague recognition. All praise should be sincere because if it is not true, then it is flattery. Flattery manipulates people's emotions because it uses empty and false praise. Praise only has meaning when it comes from someone whose opinion you value, and often, you value that person's opinion because you trust that the person is sincere.

If you are receiving praise, how you accept it matters a lot. The way to accept praise is to show that you have received and accepted it. A simple acknowledgment statement like, "Thank you, I worked hard on this one" will suffice. If other people contributed to this success, mention their names as well, and say how instrumental they were. Another critical factor is to mind your body language as you receive and acknowledge the compliment. Sit up straight, and maintain eye contact.

Run Effective Meeting

Set the table

There are great meetings and there are awful meetings. Awful gatherings ramble on always, you never appear to arrive at the point, and you leave asking why you were even present. Viable ones leave you invigorated and feeling that you've truly achieved something.

Some gatherings are a day to day lifestyle. This creates chances for effective meetings and sharing of information as well as skills.

An individual moving the motion of a particular gathering is important. This kind of gatherings are where ideas of visioning, creating networks, conceptualizing, venture planning, organizational audits, staff meetings, creation of organization visions, as well as putting objectives and activities for the employees on the memos. The factors that make the gatherings happen allow for a wide range of communication not limited to the ones mentioned.

Most individuals think that all the success of an organization can be achieved just by holding one or two gatherings while it actually takes a lot of efforts both from the administration and the employees.
Only three factors can make a meeting effective. They include:

- First of all, the planning of the meeting needs to be set and arranged in such a manner that the meeting will focus on the most pressing issues to those that do not require so much efforts.

- Oversee (and practice) your gathering presentations cautiously. You need to ensure that your members feel that their gathering has clear reason and effect.

- Keep in mind, to utilize the integrative and plural first individual of 'we' or 'us' and evade the particular 'I' with the goal that you can start to move obligation and possession to the members since they claim the outcomes.

Before your meeting: the plan.
Before you start your gathering presentation, have your room set-up to outwardly show the reason, extension, and deliverable of any workshop. In the event that you can't change over these three core values into 50 words or less (for every), at that point you are not prepared at this point to dispatch the workshop. Allow us to rehash, on the off chance that you don't have a clue what the deliverable resembles, at that point you don't have a clue what achievement resembles. Consider showing the reason, degree, and deliverable paper, alongside a lot of standard procedures proper to your governmental issues and circumstance. The accompanying gathering presentation grouping is normally ideal for a hearty beginning.
A meeting where nobody has done what they vowed to do at the last one is dead from the earliest starting point.

It's a typical enough situation, but it's one that can frequently be maintained a strategic distance from basically by ensuring that sufficient notes are circled instantly after each gathering. That way, with the talk still crisp in individuals' psyches, everybody has an unmistakable token of what they have to do. Obviously, we're not going to imagine that note composing is an exciting action, or an especially energizing part of your vocation. However, unmistakably composed, exhaustive and sorted out notes can be extremely ground-breaking. They can have the effect between the individuals who went to the gathering leaving and sitting idle, or really doing what's required so as to push a task ahead. What's more, that progress could be an immediate consequence of your notes!

Plan - Before you plan a gathering, first choose what it is you need the gathering to achieve and who should be there. A gathering is a method for passing on data—one that accommodates two-way exchange. It tends to be utilized to accumulate contribution on choices or guarantee arrangement in the working environment.

Be that as it may, in case you're giving data and not looking for exchange, a gathering may not be your most profitable technique for communication. Maybe you could send an email, or record a brisk sound or video message? Everything begins with what you need to achieve.

Planning the meeting area

The plan gives the centering structure to the gathering, places assignments in an intelligent request and time allotment, and offers a blueprint for composing the rundown report at the meeting's decision.

In the hands of a gifted facilitator, a plan ought to be viewed as a rule, not a law. Adaptability is basic to guarantee that points are settled or errands achieved in the most ideal way. Facilitators ought to envision which things could be delayed and be set up to table them until an increasingly fitting time.

The procedure plan has the extra data the facilitator and meeting pioneers need to guarantee that the gathering runs easily. Assembling the nitty gritty procedure motivation enables the gathering heads to thoroughly consider the subtleties of the whole session.

Normal room arrangement alternatives incorporate the following:

Meeting Style - Members are situated on four sides of a table. This style is frequently utilized for little board gatherings or comparable gatherings.

Square - On this particular arrangement, tables are arranged equally in sides such as that of a square hence leaving a gap in the middle. This type of sitting arrangement is important where a big number of people are expected and they need to brainstorm.

U-Shape - This particular arrangement looks like the letter U of the alphabetical order. This is more effective at gatherings that have a central source of information and hence they need to be focused to one side which in this case is the open side.

Theater Style - Columns of seats are set by one another confronting the front of the room. A speaker or moderator is at the front of the room. This style amplifies the accessible seating and functions admirably when the group of spectators needs to take negligible notes and when member collaboration will be negligible.

Study hall Style - Lines of tables face the front of the stay with two to four seats at each. This arrangement is proper when there is an introduction at the front of the room and members are relied upon to take notes.

Round Tables - Eight to ten seats are organized around little round tables. This style can be utilized for little breakout gatherings. Members can banter with one another effectively.

Figure out What You Want to Accomplish - A gathering ought to have a reason, for example, venture refreshes, exercises educated, or client criticism. On the off chance that you can't think about a reason, there might be no compelling reason to meet. "Week by week or month to month" organization gatherings, for instance, fill no need except if you know ahead of time what you need to escape each gathering occasion.

Before you plan a gathering, ask yourself: why you have to meet? Questions that can enable you to decide if a gathering is the best utilization of your or your participants' time are:

- Is there data I have to impart to participants that is mind boggling to such an extent that they should have the option to pose inquiries about it?

- Are there choices on which I need participants to give criticism?

- Are there worries that I should be certain everybody hears and sees so they can help fix them?

- Is there recognition that I need to partake before the group to propel others to perform at a more significant level?

- Are there task refreshes that colleagues need to think about, so they realize what to do straightaway?

- Does the group have data or bits of knowledge that I or others have to think about?

- Are there preparing or wellbeing methods that should be audited, refreshed or comprehended?

Set and Document an Agenda - The agenda gives the centering system to the gathering, places assignments in a legitimate request and time allotment, and offers a framework for composing the outline report at the meeting's decision.

There are regularly two renditions of an agenda. The member plan is the brief adaptation members get before a gathering. At the very least, it incorporates the gathering title, area, start and end times, goals, dialog points, also, data about how and when participants will take part. The agenda is a reasonable and streamlined variant of the itemized procedure motivation.

To help plan for your gathering, and affirm that a gathering is the best approach, build up a motivation.

You may use a motivation layout, and a model beneath to enable you to thoroughly consider your subjects. This motivation layout can be utilized to control you in arranging your gathering and thoroughly considering who needs to visit.

A meeting has to have a leader who will be responsible for the time the meeting is running. Successful meetings are fascinating, high-vitality occasions where colleagues cooperate to settle on choices or take care of issues. Shockingly, an excessive number of the gatherings we go to appear to be the exact inverse. The most noticeably awful gatherings carry time to a slither leaving everybody rationally and genuinely depleted and quite bit baffled. The thing that matters is in how the gatherings are arranged and run.

The best leader comprehends the significance of these occasions, and they comprehend that creating an incredible gathering requires arranging and intentional exertion. The following are hints to enable you to exploit this significant joint effort time with your group. Tips on the best way to fortify your meeting as a leader are as follows:

Have a Positive Attitude about Meetings

It is the absolute most significant thing a director can do as a pioneer to improve group gatherings. It's amazing what number of chiefs are glad to announce their abhorrence of gatherings, however to meet huge results, solve issues, decide, illuminate, move, team up, and inspire, directors need to work with individuals.

That is actually organizing a meeting either personally of by phone where all the individuals have to be present. Overseeing isn't tied in with sitting in the workplace with the entryway shut sending messages. As a pioneer, take a stab at taking a gander at gatherings as the sign of administration. It's authority show time, not something to fear like an outing to the dental specialist.

Keep in mind, You Own the Meeting

Try not to assign the motivation intending to a clerical specialist or another colleague. As the pioneer, it's your gathering to plan and run. To place yourself in the correct outlook, ask and answer the accompanying inquiry: "After this gathering, what will I need individuals to have learned, accomplished or fathomed?"

Request Input on the Agenda

In spite of the fact that it's the director's essential obligation to build up the motivation, colleagues can be welcome to contribute plan things. Convey a call for thoughts a couple of days before the gathering.

Allow "Blank area" for Spontaneous Creativity and Engagement

Try not to pack such a large number of things on the plan that you battle to finish it. Rather, leave some room toward the end for unconstrained talk. In the event that the gathering closes early, at that point let everybody go early. Everybody acknowledges discovered time too.

Use Team Meetings to Collaborate.

Rather than simply sharing data, take a stab at taking care of an issue or working with the gathering on landing at a choice. Indeed, it's difficult and can be chaotic, yet that is the place we get the most incentive from gatherings.

Lighten Up.

Being the pioneer of a gathering isn't tied in with parading authority or mishandling power. Berating somebody for being late before the group is a case of doing this. Keep a comical inclination and your quietude.

Be a Role Model Leader

Meetings are not a platform for you to defend yourself by discrediting others with intention to make yourself look much better than others. Try and make the meeting a general talk and more especially on the issues that relate to every person that is present in the meeting. Avoid the use of bad jokes, mockery and bad jokes as this is what distinguishes you to being a good leader and it makes the bond between everyone much stronger. Be the role model every member of the organization looks up to. Choose Who Needs to Be There- Numerous workers severely dislike going to gatherings, on the grounds that, to be honest, they're exhausting if the substance isn't applicable to the members. Along these lines, just welcome to your gathering the individuals whose info or updates you need. On the off chance that your gathering is intended to design a task, welcome the individuals who have a stake in it. In the event that the gathering is to get a choice, just welcome those whose feelings will be considered.

That may imply that you have more, however littler, gatherings. Rather than requiring a gigantic unforeseen of representatives to go to a huge group meeting, think about whether just a little piece of the motivation relates to them. Is in this way, leading a shorter gathering on simply that subject, with just the people whose info or purchase in is required on that point.

Choose a Format, Time and Location - Notwithstanding making sense of who to visit, and what you're attempting to achieve with your gathering, you'll need to pick a configuration for the gathering. For instance, in the event that you need a brisk choice that includes various individuals, a short phone meeting (telephone call) may get the job done. Inquiries regarding your gathering organization may include:

Do we have to meet face to face, up close and personal?

Does the gathering should be in private (out of earshot of others)?

Would we be able to do the gathering through phone meeting? (Or on the other hand include a telephone line so remote/voyaging members can visit?)

Would a gathering led by means of video meeting better suit our participants?

In case you're talking about delicate data or an issue that is effectively misjudged, one on one gatherings are best as they enable the gathering participants to pose inquiries and read non-verbal communication, just as hear reactions.

Maybe a few gatherings, for example, those that spread monetary data or worker changes like cutbacks, ought to be held in a private region or offsite to keep others from hearing secret data.

In the event that your group is remote, the best configuration might be a video meeting. That decreases travel and can get everybody in the equivalent "room" a lot quicker. Your gathering arrangement can be added to your motivation layout with the goal that everybody on the welcome rundown knows about how you intend to meet.

Welcome Attendees - Before holding the meeting it is polite to chat while you wait for the meeting to begin. It would be better to discuss things unrelated to the meeting, such as weather, family or weekend plans. Once everyone arrives, you should formally welcome everyone to the meeting and thank the participants for coming.

If the meeting is a small group, it is probably not necessary to take the participation out loud. You will know everyone personally and can indicate who is present and who is absent. In a larger meeting, you may need to send an attendance sheet or call names.

Effective Written Communication

Like many other forms of communication, written communication gets taken for granted all the time.

We write and send messages everyday almost instinctively without thinking about the nature of our communication. More often if we have an idea of the message we need to convey, we write it and send it.

Written communication might come so easily to many people, but it is not always a walk in the park. There are many instances, especially in formal situations where you come across emails that are so poorly written that you struggle to understand what the intention was. In such messages, it is impossible to find the information you need. Most of such communication is riddled with incomplete sentences, wrong spellings and other grammatical errors.

By the time you deduce the objectives from such communication, you end up spending more time than you have to. It is also possible that you might not even make sense of the communication at all.

Poorly written communication has dire effects. If, for example, you receive an email notifying you of a meeting however, the structure of that email is so confusing that you barely understand the objectives.

By the time you go to the meeting, you are not well-prepared for the agenda because you spent most of your time trying to understand the communiqué.

A lot of people have been in such situations with written communication before. It might not be in an official capacity, but you have experienced the challenges associated with poorly written communication from time to time.

There is a lot of information overload in the world and to overcome the challenges that this brings, it is important to learn how to communicate better, effectively, and provide clear and concise instructions.

If you are sending an official email, remember that no one in an official capacity has the time to go through all of the five book-length pages you are writing. It gets worse when the structure is poor.

Written skills are a prerequisite in almost all formal settings. Even in personal communication, these skills are healthy as they will help you communicate better and avoid conflict as a result of misunderstandings. Properly written communication also helps you create a lasting impression on the people around you. They get used to your communication skills and in some cases, will always look forward to reading something from you.

Great writing skills can help you create a harmonious relationship with people in your corporate circle, and you might even be called upon to write speeches. Communication, therefore, is more than just writing some words and hitting send.

Understanding the Audience

Don't be selfish. When writing a message, do not only focus on what you want, what works for you and the response you expect from the recipient.

This is where many people go wrong. Communication goes full circle when the message is clear and the recipient acknowledges receipt and comprehension. Without that, your message could mean anything.

The first step to improving your written communication is to think about the audience. Concerning the audience, there are a lot of things you can look at.

First, what kind of message are you sending? Is it a formal or informal email? Whichever of these two you choose, there are written and unwritten guidelines that will help you write the message and achieve your intended purpose with minimal discomfort.

What about the time? When is the appropriate time to send the message? These days companies have done a lot of research on this, and they choose appropriate times from research to send emails to customers detailing different objectives. You should also do the same.

Consider the position of your recipient relative to the time. If you need an urgent response, sending the message when you know the recipient is held up would be absurd.

Each setting, formal or informal, has a unique writing format you should adhere to.

The format helps you ensure your correspondence does not look odd and awkward. Imagine sending your parents an email but starting it with Dear Sir/Madam. While they might read the email, they will feel something is not right, unless it was a prank and you reveal it in the letter. The format used in the letter also involves thinking about the tone in your message. You can set the tone based on the specific words you use.

The reader picks up on those words and understands the urgency of the message or any other intended learning point.

Therefore, it is always a good idea to think about your audience and use that knowledge to influence your written message.

Choosing the Correct Style

Since you are already aware of the demographics of your audience, the next step is to get busy. If you are typing your message on a computer, getting started is not one of the easiest things. You can end up staring at that blank emptiness for a long time without making any progress.

To get started, ask yourself what you want the audience to know about. After all, they are not in control, you are. They don't know the information you are about to share with them. Come up with an outline. The outline acts as a guide for you especially when you are working on a long document like a speech, presentation or a report.

An outline helps you create clear talking points, come up with steps to follow to ensure your message is concise and leaves no doubt in the minds of the reader.

It is easy to talk about empathy in verbal communication, but most people struggle to implement it in written communication. Empathizing in written communication is a skill that, once mastered, can help you interact with different people of diverse needs. Empathizing in your correspondence helps the recipient understand why they need to think about your message and why it is important. You should strive to address their needs.

Another important element in the style of your composition is choosing the right theme. What message should resonate in the minds of your readers when they go through your email?

In case you are unsure how to go about this, imagine you have twenty seconds to explain your email to someone.

What would you talk about? What is the subject and what are the major talking points? Your answer to this should guide you on the theme of your message.

Effective Public Speaking

Powerful Public Speaking is a significant expertise in imparting learning and communicating thoughts to gatherings of individuals. It is an essential mechanism for introducing and selling your items and thoughts. Having the option to verbally impart adequately to different people or to gatherings is fundamental in school, business, just as your own life.

There is a requirement for individuals who can viably make introductions and address others. Your insight and aptitudes around there can help advance your profession or improve your business. Likewise, on the off chance that you are great or truly appreciate public speaking, you may even pick speaking as a calling. Gifted Public Speaker will get the thing going notwithstanding during the hour of emergency. Numerous speakers have achieved extraordinary changes by the sheer impact of their successful talks. You also can be one of those rare sorts of people who have deserted a trail of history which will keep them in the recollections of the ages to come.

You can figure out how to turn into an increasingly viable speaker by utilizing the correct methods and rehearsing your public speaking aptitudes. Here are a few systems to pursue:

1. Care About Your Theme

Enthusiasm goes far with regards to being a successful speaker. The group of spectators can tell in case you're emotionless. In the event that you couldn't care less, they won't mind either. Much more dreadful, you can appear to be a phony.

Then again, in the event that you earnestly care about your theme, the group of spectators will get on that as well. They'll see you as being progressively true and trustworthy. They'll listen all the more near find why your subject is so critical to you. Furthermore, they're bound to pardon any minor errors you may make.

2. Keep in mind Your Speaking Objective

We've all likely tuned in to at any rate one speaker who appeared to continue endlessly always about nothing specifically. One motivation behind why this happens is on the grounds that the discourse isn't centered enough. The speaker is attempting to cover excessively and winds up exhausting their audience members.

Right off the bat during the time spent building up your discourse, distinguish the motivation behind why you're speaking. Make it a point to adhere to this objective during your introduction. Try not to get derailed off-subject.

3. Bolster Your Central matters

Each point you make in your discourse should be bolstered with either a model, a representation, or certainties. When you're supporting a point, it's ideal to be as explicit as you can be.

For instance, in a discourse about the significance of clean water this announcement is excessively ambiguous:

"Numerous individuals don't have clean water."

Expressing this measurement from the U.S. Community for Sickness Control is an increasingly successful approach to help your point:

"Around the world, 780 million individuals don't approach an improved water source."

4. Recount to a Story

Individuals love a decent story. Along these lines, on the off chance that you need to be a progressively powerful speaker, recount to a story.

Narrating is an incredible method to make your material additionally captivating and to identify with your crowd. Ensure your story is relatable and important.

In case you're speaking is about your business, here are a few instances of stories you might most likely tell:

- A client story. The account of how your item or administrations addressed an issue for a particular client or tackled an issue. Fulfilled clients are regularly glad to share this.
- Your organization story. The narrative of how your organization became. This can be particularly compelling if it's client situated.

- An item advancement story. The account of how you came to offer another item.

Obviously, there are numerous different sorts of stories you could tell contingent upon the kind of speaking you are doing.

5. Use Introduction Instruments Shrewdly Slide introductions regularly get a notoriety for being dull, however, that is on the grounds that numerous speakers are uninformed of what their introduction devices can do and don't utilize every one of the highlights. To more readily draw in your group of spectators, figure out how to utilize the further developed highlights of your device.

For instance, here are only a couple of ways you can utilize PowerPoint and Google Slides (with connections to related instructional exercises):

- Add movements (PowerPoint, Google Slides)
- Add video (PowerPoint, Google Slides)
- Add sound (PowerPoint, Google Slides)
- Construct a timetable (PowerPoint, Google Slides)

Furthermore, these highlights are only a hint of something larger. To truly lift your public speaking procedures, you'll need to get the hang of everything your introduction programming instrument can do.

6. Utilize an Expert Layout

While we're discussing introduction devices, we should likewise discuss the introduction plan. Your introduction configuration influences how your group of spectators sees you. Regardless of whether you've retained your discourse, give it flawlessly, and have the most astounding theme - your group of spectators may even now pass judgment on you contrarily if your introduction configuration is messy and amateurish.

Obviously, you could utilize a standard layout (similar ones that everybody uses) or structure your own format (exorbitant and tedious). In any case, a superior arrangement is to utilize an expertly planned introduction format that you can without much of a stretch tweak. The introduction formats from Envato Components and GraphicRiver, for instance, are demonstrated, simple to-utilize, and proficient. Also, there are hundreds to browse - so you will undoubtedly discover one that addresses your issues.

Pace Yourself

With regards to public speaking, a typical novice mistake is to talk too rapidly. This is generally brought about by a mix of nerves and not understanding how quick you're really speaking. Be that as it may, talking too quickly makes it harder for your audience members to comprehend what you're stating.

Compelling public speakers know to pace themselves. They'll talk at a characteristic pace and work short, normal delays into their discourse.

It likewise encourages on the off chance that you make sure to inhale during your discourse. An astonishing number of individuals hold their breath without acknowledging it when they're anxious (I'm one of them). In any case, holding your breath will just build your tension. Thus, make sure to inhale profoundly during the breaks in your discourse. On the off chance that your discourse is a long one, taking a taste of water throughout a break can likewise help.

Include Visual Guides

Visual guides can fill in as an incredible representation of your discourse. People utilize their sight more than some other sense. In this way, on the off chance that you can come to your meaningful conclusion by indicating it to your audience members as opposed to portraying it, they are bound to recall it.

Be cautious, however. To be powerful, your visual guide must be of high caliber and effectively unmistakable to all individuals from your group of spectators. Abstain from fusing messy designs into a slide introduction. In like manner, don't hold up a visual guide that is physically unreasonably little for those tuning in to see.

Dress Easily, Yet Expertly

What's the correct outfit to wear in the event that you need to be a successful public speaker?

All things considered, there's nobody answer. How you dress relies upon who your audience members will be. Yet, the general guideline is that you need to dress expertly to establish a decent connection. Try to watch great prepping and cleanliness leads as well. Numerous specialists feel you should dress as indicated by how your group of spectators dresses. In the event that the crowd is dressed officially, you would prefer not to appear in shorts and a tee-shirt. Similarly, if the group of spectators is wearing shorts and a tee-shirt, don't dress officially.

Maintain a Strategic Distance from Unbalanced Fillers

"Um," "uh," "like." We as a whole slip these filler words into our discussions without acknowledging it. In any case, abuse of these words during an expert discourse can make you sound not exactly sure. In the event that you can, get out from under the propensity for utilizing these words to improve as a public speaker.

Practice can enable you to kill these words from your discourse designs, however, you might be so used to utilizing them that it's difficult to see when you're doing it. This is the place a discourse mentor, instructor, or companion would prove to be useful. They could tune in for these words and help you get out from under the propensity for utilizing them.

Use Motions (Yet Don't Exaggerate)

Characteristic development during a discourse is an indication of a successful public speaker. Hand motions and notwithstanding making a couple of strides over the stage can be great public speaking strategies insofar as they're regular, intentional, and not exaggerated. Development can cause you to show up increasingly agreeable and help your group of spectators identify with you. You've presumably observed the hardened speaker who conveys their discourse while standing stock still, hands hanging flaccidly close by. Which would you rather tune in to? That firm speaker, or a speaker who intersperses their discourse every once in a while with important hand signals?

Permit Questions and Answers

Question and answer sessions (question and answer) are one of the most underused public speaking strategies. Numerous speakers simply state what they're going to state and after that plunk down. What a waste!

The excellence of question and answer is that you get the opportunity to hear your audience members' worries straightforwardly and address them publicly, further fortifying your case.

You can get ready for a question and answer session by making your very own rundown of inquiries and potential complaints that crowd individuals may have (with answers). Concentrate the rundown cautiously so you're comfortable with it. On the off chance that somebody brings up a point that you hadn't thought of, don't freeze. They don't anticipate that you should know it all. It's splendidly worthy to take their contact data and reveal to them that you'll hit them up once you have the appropriate response.

Conclusion

Communication, first of all, is an attitude of openness to the other, which implies generous availability to share, that is, to give and receive.

However, this is not easy; It is an art that must be practiced continuously to develop it in all its fullness and thus be able to obtain the best benefit from it. We as human beings need to practice to the fullest and improve the quality of our communication every day.

And we talk about quality when we mean that we are called to share with other people not only the things we do during the day and what we have learned, but to go deeper to ourselves. The one who truly wants to communicate knows how to listen, including silence, because it is also part of the communication. An open ear is the only reliable sign of an open heart. And listening constitutes ninety percent of good communication because we all desperately need to be heard.

This also constitutes a fundamental element in all social life. If it is deleted in a group, it will cease to exist as such.

If you want to have greater productivity in an organization, you must have a good communication system and to achieve this the expert must consider the context of the recipient or audiences to whom they are addressed, taking into account their ideas, values, knowledge in the subject , situation with respect to the organization (position within the organization chart if it is an internal or external public), its image of it, cultural level, etc. and value the knowledge and importance of an expert in the area of communication.

The person responsible for managing the communication system of a company must analyze all these aspects, but above all, it must know the nature, uses, characteristics, advantages, disadvantages of each of the means of communication available in the market and use the appropriate means for each situation, if you do the above, you will achieve effective communication and, consequently, the objectives set out will be carried out satisfactorily.

Effective communication is essential in any workplace. When a company has people that practice effective communication skills, working relationships are better and productivity is higher. Employees tend to respect leaders that can communicate well with their subordinates, and people in middle management appreciate subordinates than can effectively communicate their concerns.

With the existence of effective communication in the workplace, hostile working environments are avoided. Colleagues gain respect for each other, and interactions with bosses, subordinates or colleagues become pleasant and enjoyable. This contributes to the happiness of employees with their jobs and the company that they work for. Believe it or not, employees tend to value their happiness in the workplace more than their salary because, although money is important for all employees, happiness in their jobs and workplaces is deemed more essential.

Communication is important in all aspects of life. Whether you want to promote yourself, win new friends, or just share a common experience with someone new; learning how to communicate effectively is the best way to enhance your world.

Learning the right way to communicate in every situation is challenging and takes time to grasp. The good news is that the more you practice, the easier communication is. Don't give up if you have a few negative interactions.

CPSIA information can be obtained
at www.ICGtesting.com
Printed in the USA
BVHW011007120521
606930BV00012B/55